Relationship Secrets
of
Pride and Prejudice

A BIBLE STUDY
BASED ON LESSONS FOUND
IN THE BELOVED CLASSIC

Chrisann Dawson

Visit Shine-A-Light Press on their website: www.ShineALightPress.com
and on Twitter: @SALPress

The Shine-A-Light Press logo is a trademark of Shine-A-Light Corp.

Relationship Secrets *of* Pride and Prejudice © 2021 by Chrisann Dawson
All rights reserved. Published by Shine-A-Light Press.

Shine-A-Light Press and associated logos are trademarks and/or are registered trademarks of Shine-A-Light Corp. No part of this publication may be reproduced, stored in a retrieval system, or transmitted in any form or by any means, electronic, mechanical, photocopying, recording, or otherwise without the written permission of Shine-A-Light Corp.
For information regarding permission, please contact the permissions department at
info@shinealightcorp.com.

Scripture taken from The ESV® Bible (The Holy Bible, English Standard Version®), copyright © 2001 by Crossway, a publishing ministry of Good News Publishers. Used by permission. All rights reserved.

This resource is intended for individual use only.

Edits and book design by Andrea Elston.

ISBN 978-1-953158-07-9

DEDICATION

This book is dedicated to the wisdom of Jane Austen and all who love her writings.

CONTENTS

	Author's Note	pg. 1
1	Week One: *cast of minor characters*	pg. 3
2	Week Two: *the backstory*	pg. 14
3	Week Three: *secret #1~faithful love*	pg. 21
4	Week Four: *secret #2~a willingness to grow*	pg. 33
5	Week Five: *secret #3~respect*	pg. 43
6	Week Six: *secret #4~confession*	pg. 53
7	Week Seven: *secret #5~gratitude*	pg. 66
8	Conclusion	pg. 77

A NOTE FROM THE AUTHOR

Can one truly find relationship secrets in the tale of <u>Pride and Prejudice</u> by Jane Austen? Is it accurate to call these foundational principles "secrets"? Perhaps. Many have simply read through the novel, enjoying the development of the characters, and the sequence of events, without grasping the underlying truths embedded throughout it.

This book will take a closer look at these life-supporting moorings found in Jane Austen's novel, primarily focusing on the examples to emulate. But first, let's get the bad news out of the way. The author also lays open to ridicule the irritating examples of those to be scorned: the relationship between Mr. and Mrs. Bennet, the marriage of Mr. Collins and Charlotte Lucas, the impact of Mr. Wickham's selfishness on everyone around him, and finally the backstory of Mr. Darcy and Elizabeth Bennet's rocky start.

I hope you find this study a beautiful blend of educational, inspirational, and enjoyable! Enjoy with me the exploring of these timeless characters and learn with me how to laugh at their foibles, learn from their mistakes, and emulate their strengths.
Some sections are longer than others based on the flow of the novel itself. Feel free to break up the study as best fits your schedule or your group.

Chrisann Dawson

WEEK ONE

CAST OF MINOR CHARACTERS

Mr. and Mrs. Bennet

Mr. Collins and Charlotte Lucas

Mr. George Wickham and Lydia Bennet

Although these characters are not the main players in the story of Pride and Prejudice, there are still valuable lessons to be learned from these irreputable relationships. Let's take a look.

Mr. and Mrs. Bennet

Mr. Bennet, initially attracted to youthful beauty and an outgoing personality, married a foolish woman. Mrs. Bennet, aside from her goal of seeing her five daughters well married, lived in the small world of pleasing herself. Mr. Bennet, a well-educated country gentleman, was forced to tolerate his wife's folly on a daily basis for their more than twenty years of marriage.

Mr. Bennet's lesson: *practice tolerance*, even though *he* did it through humor.

1 Corinthians 13:4 advises: "Love is patient." In an alternate version, it says "Love suffers long." Mr. Bennet, for more than twenty years of marriage, had to put up with the folly of his wife. She was so foolish that she rarely realized that she was the object of his sarcasm. Still, he practiced patience with her. He had chosen beauty over wisdom and paid a heavy price.

Look up **Ephesians 4:2 and fill in the blanks**. This verse praises four qualities:

1. humility   2. _____

3. patience   4. _____

Can you think of ways that Mr. Bennet practices these qualities? Describe how Mr. Bennet shows specifically gentleness and patience with his family.

_____

_____

_____

Why is it important to wisely choose who you will partner with in life?

_____

_____

_____

What are some qualities in a person that you admire? How do those qualities support a strong marriage?

_____

_____

_____

Are you, or do you think you will be, as tolerant of your life's partner as Mr. Bennet is of his? How is patience truly an act of love?

_____

_____

_____

Mrs. Bennet's lesson: *value wisdom as a woman.*

Proverbs 31: 30 concludes, "Charm is deceitful, and beauty is vain, but a woman who fears the LORD is to be praised." Mrs. Bennet's pursuit of husbands for her five daughters often prompted her to behave foolishly. May we favor wisdom and reverence for God over ambition and folly.

Proverbs 29:11 shares, "A fool gives full vent to his spirit, but a wise man quietly holds it back." Mrs. Bennet is so foolish that she openly gives vent to her folly. Do you think that Mrs. Bennet is aware of her own indiscretions? How would *you* advise Mrs. Bennet to behave when it came to seeing her daughters happily married?

_____

_____

_____

Mr. Collins and Charlotte Lucas

Mr. Collins was a simple-minded, self-centered young man, who had the opportunity to think highly of himself because he had been commissioned to a pastorate which came with a beautiful cottage. He considered himself a great catch. Mr. Bennet had inherited his estate, Longbourn, through the legal process called an entail. The property needed to pass to a male heir, the said Mr. Collins. Mr. Collins hopes to bridge the rift with the Bennet family by marrying one of the daughters. When

Elizabeth turns him down, he aims his love at his next target, Charlotte Lucas.

Charlotte was seven years older than Elizabeth and was quickly becoming a spinster. Not willing to be poor and single forever, Charlotte embraced what Elizabeth rejected, namely an opportunity to marry a foolish man and gain a secure home.

Mr. Collins' lesson: *think less often of self.*

Mr. Collins only, ever thought of himself, his accomplishments, and his agendas. But **Philippians 2:4** states, "Let each of you look not only to his own interests, but also to the interests of others." Mr. Collins assumed he would be a great catch. He assumed that Elizabeth would only see his value. Let us all be *less* like Mr. Collins.

1 John 4:7 says, "Beloved, let us love one another, for love is of God…" Although Mr. Collins is in ministry and should know better, he only seems to love himself. Have you ever known someone like Mr. Collins who only cared for himself (or herself)? If you are comfortable, write their name here:

_____

What advice would you give Mr. Collins on having a happy and loving marriage?

_____

_____

_____

Charlotte Lucas' lesson: *trust God to supply.*

Charlotte was willing to sacrifice a lifetime of living with a foolish man for the security of a home and provision. Proverbs 23:4 says, "Do not toil to acquire wealth; be discerning enough to desist." Charlotte was not duped into marrying Mr. Collins, a foolish, selfish man, but rather she walked into the relationship with her eyes wide open, willing to pay a steep price for financial peace of mind.

Look up Philippians 4:19 and write it here: _____

_____

Is Charlotte Lucas trusting God to take care of her financial needs? _____

What is one need that you have a particularly hard time trusting that God will provide? _____

We know the promises in God's Word are always true, but share a time when God took care of a need for you and made Philippians 4:19 feel especially true.

_____

_____

_____

_____

In that era, women had few options for financial security. Would you be willing, like Charlotte Lucas, to trade your peace for a lifetime of security? Why or why not?

_____

_____

_____

Do you blame Charlotte Lucas for her decision? Explain your reasoning.

_____

_____

Mr. George Wickham and Lydia Bennet

Mr. Wickham could be held up as one of literature's perfect examples of the selfish, self-serving man; for that he certainly was. Sadly, Elizabeth's foolish younger sister, Lydia, lacks wisdom. Wickham successfully lures Lydia into a relationship with no assurance of marriage in the hopes of manipulating her family for money. Only Mr. Darcy, and his motive of faithful love for Elizabeth, has the power and means to correct Lydia's glaring mistake and make her honorable once again. Mr. Darcy pays all Wickham's debts and anonymously arranges for a dowry for Lydia as well as a new commission for Wickham, just to give them a fresh start.

Mr. Wickham's lesson: *do not employ deceit to gain favor.*

At his earliest opportunity, George Wickham turns Elizabeth against Mr. Darcy by telling her a false story of how Darcy had not honored his father's dying wish to provide for Wickham. **1 Peter 2:1** admonishes, "Put away all malice and all deceit and hypocrisy and envy and all slander." In a bid to make himself look like the victim, Wickham turned Elizabeth against Darcy. He later used these same practices to woo Elizabeth's foolish younger sister, Lydia, into a relationship. Wickham is all about being self-serving and deceitful.

Read **Proverbs 12:19**. What type of words last forever? _____

What type of words lasting only for a moment? _____

Have you ever known a self-serving and/or deceitful person? If you feel comfortable, write their name here: _____

How did people respond to his (or her) self-centeredness? Did their reaction surprise you or was it as expected?

_____

_____

_____

Lydia Bennet's lesson: *honor and family are more valuable than ambition.*

Lydia, who only ever thought of herself and her own fun, was easily tricked by Wickham into a relationship with no promise of marriage. His aim was to use her to gain money from the Bennet family. **Proverbs 17:25** sadly shares, "A foolish son is a grief to his father and bitterness to her who bore him." The same, of course, can be said about daughters. Lydia cared more for herself than her family or reputation. Only Mr. Darcy, prompted by love for Elizabeth, could fix the mess she made.

Look up **1 Corinthians 13: 5**. Speaking of love, it says, "It does not insist on its own _____." Lydia insisted always on having her own way. What advice would you give her to be careful of Wickham and not so easily succumb to his wiles? Write a letter (or a text) warning her of what may come from pursuing this relationship.

_____

_____

_____

_____

_____

Do you think you would be wiser than Elizabeth Bennet? Would you see through Wickham's lies and realize that you were being manipulated? Why or why not?

_____

_____

_____

Would you be as foolish as Lydia Bennet? Would you allow your reputation to be stained in order to have fun and your own way?

The Bennet's, Charlotte Lucas and Mr. Collins, and George Wickham and Lydia Bennet are all flawed characters in this tale. But before we move on, let's take a look at how Elizabeth Bennet and Mr. Darcy started their relationship on such a rocky footing.

WEEK TWO

THE BACKSTORY

Mr. Darcy and Elizabeth Bennet

Before I can plunge into exploring the relationship "secrets" found in this tale, I must delve a bit into the reasons why Elizabeth Bennet and Mr. Fitzwilliam Darcy began their relationship with such a horrible start. And I really hate to pour the blame heavily on Mr. Darcy, but I feel he has a strong enough personality to shoulder that burden.

Mr. Bingley is only mildly handsome but has incredible manners. Mr. Darcy is incredibly handsome but lacks the gentlemanly manners of his friend. But Darcy's good looks diminished in the light of his excessive pride. At an assembly ball, Darcy turns down an opportunity to meet and dance with Elizabeth. Charles Bingley urges his friend, Darcy, to dance. "Darcy, I must have you dance. I hate to see you standing by yourself in this stupid manner." Bingley asks his friend to dance with Elizabeth. In Elizabeth's earshot, Mr. Darcy replied to his friend Bingley: "She is tolerable; but not handsome enough to tempt me. And I am in no humor to give consequence to young ladies who are slighted by other men."

What does the first part of **Ephesians 4:32** state? "Be kind one to another, _____,..." Mr. Darcy is far from kind at his first opportunity to meet Elizabeth Bennet. Mr. Darcy's friend, Charles Bingley, is not as handsome nor as rich, but his manners are open, humble, and kind. Darcy's riches and good looks faded as his proud attitude became evident. Elizabeth laughed off the wound but remembered the slight.

Are you generally considered to be kind and tenderhearted? Are there areas where you are snobby like Mr. Darcy? (Now is the time to be honest with yourself!) _____ What is your best advice for both Elizabeth and Mr. Darcy in this circumstance?

_____

_____

_____

The second part of **Ephesians 4:32** could advise Elizabeth here: "_____ one another, as God in Christ forgave you." Although he wasn't sorry for his snobbery till much later in the story, Mr. Darcy still could have been forgiven by Elizabeth for the wounds he caused her. Very often, we are asked to forgive even though the offender isn't sorry. Put yourself in Miss Bennet's shoes. Would you have forgiven Mr. Darcy more freely than Elizabeth? _____ On a scale of one to ten, how difficult is it to forgive someone who is not sorry? Circle one:

1   2   3   4   5   6   7   8   9   10

impossible   easy

Share a time when you were able to forgive even though the offender was not sorry for the wound that was caused.

_____

_____

_____

_____

Through no fault of her own, Elizabeth was hurt by Mr. Darcy on their first opportunity to meet and get to know one another. A few weeks later, when she had the opportunity to listen to maligning gossip about Darcy from Wickham, she latched onto it with little discernment. Wickham falsely claimed that Darcy purposefully caused his poverty by ignoring his dying father's wishes.

Proverbs 16:28 reminds us that, "A dishonest man spreads strife, and a whisperer separates close friends." Elizabeth Bennet's wound from Darcy speaks to her normally wise mind and causes her to fall prey to Wickham's malicious gossip about Mr. Darcy.

If Darcy had not caused that first hurt, do you think Elizabeth would have been tricked by George Wickham and his selfish lie? _____

Why or why not? _____

_____

Have you ever permitted an unresolved wound to cloud your judgment about someone? Share this and how you overcame it.

_____

_____

_____

_____

_____

A third offense was Darcy's eventual interference in the relationship between Elizabeth's sister Jane and Charles Bingley. Charles Bingley, Darcy's close friend, had grown very much in love with Jane Bennet, courting her in the style of the age. Although Bingley loved Jane enough to want to propose, Darcy stepped in to discourage him.

What does **Colossians 3:12** say? "Put on then, as God's chosen ones, holy and beloved, _____ hearts, kindness, _____, meekness, and _____. "Mr. Darcy's interference stemmed from pride and not humility. A humble person views himself as no different than his fellow humans. Mr. Darcy allowed his family pride to disdain the Bennet family, not only for himself, but also for his friend. Have you ever met or known someone filled with pride as a result of the worth or reputation of their family? If yes, can you share how this person was perceived by others around him (or her).

_____

_____

_____

1 Thessalonians 4:11 encourages, "...aspire to live quietly, and to mind your own affairs..." Mr. Darcy pompously separates his friend, Charles Bingley, from Elizabeth's sister Jane because he feels like the Bennet family is beneath them.

How should have Mr. Darcy behaved concerning his friend and Jane Bennet?

_____

_____

_____

Have you ever had someone officiously interfere in your life? Share the story and how you managed it.

_____

_____

_____

_____

Am I unfair in accusing Mr. Darcy of beginning the rocky relationship with Elizabeth? I think not.

    As the story progresses, Mr. Darcy gradually changes his opinion of Elizabeth, not realizing that her thoughts of him remained rooted in that early bitterness, the gossip from Mr. Wickham, and Darcy's eventual interference in the relationship between her sister Jane and Bingley. The first proposal, one of the most admired scenes in the tale, was completely one-sided: love on Darcy's part, but only disgust and disdain from Elizabeth, thus the title <u>Pride and Prejudice</u>.

Colossians 3:13 says, "…bearing with one another and, if one has a complaint against another, forgiving each other; as the Lord has forgiven you, so you must also forgive." Mr. Darcy forgot what he originally disliked about Elizabeth Bennet, but Elizabeth did not forget the offenses of Mr. Darcy. At his first proposal, she turns him down flat.

Do you understand Elizabeth's need to hang on to her wounds? Share a time when someone hurt you and you struggled to forgive.

_____

_____

_____

Do you feel as if Elizabeth's initial rejection of Darcy's proposal is poetic justice? _____ Why is it that we crave seeing justice done?

_____

_____

_____

Let's study some relationship secrets from <u>Pride and Prejudice</u> that made the difference and changed the tide of emotions and eventually the outcome of the novel.

WEEK THREE

SECRET #1 ~ FAITHFUL LOVE

How could the first "secret" available to the careful reader of <u>Pride and Prejudice</u> be anything but faithful, enduring love? Despite Mr. Darcy's pride and original disdain of Elizabeth Bennet, time and opportunity in her presence changes his mind. He begins to love her. His love grows so gradually that it surprises even him when he realizes it.

Song of Solomon 8:6 proclaims, "-love is strong as death…" As strong as death is to separate, love is stronger. Love can eternally join and unite. And because of the power of love, Mr. Darcy, despite his early faults and errors, has developed a strong and passionate regard for Elizabeth Bennet.

How has love proven itself to be strong in your life?

_____

_____

_____

_____

Those who love this tale love the first time Mr. Darcy proposes to Elizabeth Bennet; the time he tries really hard and fails really miserably to secure Elizabeth's hand in marriage.

Mr. Darcy meets up with Elizabeth Bennet in Hunsford when she is visiting her friend Charlotte who had married Elizabeth's cousin, Mr. Collins. Mr. Collins is a parson on the property of Mr. Darcy's very rich aunt, Lady Catherine de Bourgh. Elizabeth had planned a long six-week visit, and since the parson's family dined often with their wealthy neighbor, Mr. Darcy had a long time to firmly change his opinion in favor of Elizabeth Bennet. Even before parting with her in the late fall, Darcy realized he was in danger of falling in love with this woman whom he considered below him in station.

Write **Proverbs 16:18** here: _____

_____

Early in the story of <u>Pride and Prejudice</u>, Mr. Darcy's pride was often talked of. Despite his growing love for Elizabeth Bennet, he still considers her family as beneath him.

How can this type of pride or conceit hinder a loving relationship?

_____

_____

_____

Proverbs 18:12 starts out, "Before destruction a man's heart is haughty…" Although being rejected by Elizabeth at that first proposal is hardly destruction, it did have the power to transform his outlook and personality. If you have ever been humbled by a difficult circumstance, share this experience and what you learned from it.

_____

_____

_____

_____

Galatians 6:3 offers this reminder, "For if anyone thinks that he is something, when he is nothing, deceives himself." Although Mr. Darcy had many reasons to believe himself a great catch for someone from Elizabeth's class, his simple arrogance *was* the turn off. Have you ever known someone who thought that he (or she) was above the average person? If you feel comfortable, write their name here: _____

How did others relate to that person?

_____

_____

_____

Did that person ever learn to think more honestly about himself?

_____

When Elizabeth comes down with a severe headache upon learning that Mr. Darcy had separated her sister Jane from Mr. Bingley, Darcy is worried for her health and pays a visit. Confident in who he is, confident that he is an excellent catch for someone from Elizabeth's class in society, Mr. Darcy declared his love to Elizabeth with intense passion. Thankfully, his strong love was expressed before he began to destroy his chances.

Author Jane Austen shared that Mr. Darcy's "tenderness morphed into hints at his pride: he recognized her inferiority, and when he dwelt on her family's obstacles, his speech was warm but wounding. He was not recommending himself well to Elizabeth."

James 4:17 warns, "So whoever knows the right thing to do and fails to do it, for him it is sin." Although Mr. Darcy was trained as a child by his parents to practice good manners, his adult person had forgotten their importance.

If Mr. Darcy had used good manners in his proposal, do you think that he would have been so transparent with Elizabeth? _____ How would you advise Mr. Darcy on the art of the successful proposal?

_____

_____

_____

_____

Originally, Elizabeth feels guilty about the pain her rejection was going to cause Darcy. Quickly though her guilt changed to anger as he continued to explain why he was stooping so low to ask her to marry him. Her answer was straight-forward: "I believe the established mode is to express a sense of obligation for the compliment of your proposal. If I could feel gratitude, I would now thank you. But I cannot-I have never desired your good opinion, and you have bestowed most unwillingly. I hope your pain will be of short duration, but I cannot accept your proposal."

Proverbs 29:11 states, "A fool gives full vent to his spirit, but a wise man quietly holds it back."

Today's society touts the benefits of being completely honest. But Scripture encourages us to not share everything that we are thinking.

Do you think that Darcy and Elizabeth should have practiced restraint? _____ Are there relationships in your life that could benefit from restraint? Explain and share.

_____

_____

_____

_____

The author said: "It was obvious that Mr. Darcy was shocked with surprise. His complexion became pale with anger. He struggled for composure and would not open his lips until he believed he had attained it." He went on to demand an explanation to Elizabeth's curt rejection.

Elizabeth lays two heavy charges against Mr. Darcy: one was that he had separated her sister Jane from the man she loved, Darcy's friend, Charles Bingley; the second charge was that he had purposefully brought George Wickham to his current state of poverty intentionally. Instead of immediately defending himself, he listens to her charges and then dismissed himself: "You have said quite enough, madam. I perfectly comprehend your feelings, and I have now only to be ashamed of what my own have been. Forgive me for taking up so much of your time and accept my wishes for your health and happiness." With that he leaves Elizabeth stunned and breathless.

Romans 8:33 wonders, "Who shalll bring _____ __ _____

_____ God's elect?" When surprised that any intelligent woman would turn down his proposal, Mr. Darcy asks for an explanation for Elizabeth's rejection. She levels two accusations at him. Both serious. The charge of separating Bingley and Jane was brought out of love for a sister, but the charge of causing Wickham's poverty was based only on gossip.

Do you blame Elizabeth for turning down Mr. Darcy? _____
Would you have turned down such a proposal? _____ Have you ever falsely accused someone of something or been accused? _____
If you cans share the story and how you overcame the problem.

_____

_____

_____

_____

_____

Elizabeth spent a sleepless night thinking over the strange and painful proposal, and the next morning is handed a letter by Mr. Darcy to explain his side of her accusations.

Initially reluctant to even open the letter, Elizabeth allowed curiosity to lead her. It began: "Be not alarmed, Madam, that this letter has a renewal of offers which last night were so disgusting to you. Two offenses of a very different nature, you laid to my charge last night, that of separating Bingley from your sister, and my treatment of Mr. Wickham. Let me defend myself on both."

Mr. Darcy began with his reasons for separating his friend, Charles Bingley, from Elizabeth's older sister, Jane. Simply, he believed that Bingley was more emotionally attached to Jane than she had been to him. Of course, he must recognize the inferiority of the Bennet family, not just financially, but in the crudeness of manners of Mrs. Bennet and the two younger Bennet sisters, Catherine and Lydia. Mrs. Bennet had been overhead by Mr. Darcy, on the night of that last ball, bragging upon the soon to be event of an engagement between Mr. Bingley and Jane. It was Darcy's first realization of how serious his friend was in his relationship and how precarious it was to allow him to be joined with a family of such low connections. Along with Mr. Bingley's sisters, Mr. Darcy convinced Bingley that Jane did not truly love him; the very next day, they whisked him off to London. In his letter, Darcy barely excused this interference, simply claiming that he did not perceive Jane to be as much in love with Bingley, as he was with her. Darcy's only regret was not telling Bingley that Jane had been in London for an extended visit. He confessed his lie by omission as beneath him.

Please write **Matthew 7:12** here: _____

_____

This verse is often called the Golden Rule. Instead of being kind, Mr. Darcy officiously interfered in the relationship of his friend with Jane Bennet, Elizabeth's older sister. He separated them because he thought the Bennet family was beneath his friend. He even hinted that he was lowering himself to propose to Elizabeth.

Is Elizabeth right for being angry with Darcy? _____ Do you blame Darcy for not following the Golden Rule and interfering in his friend's relationship? _____ How does practicing the Golden Rule (treating others like you would like to be treated) prevent poor decisions, like that of Darcy to be a busybody?

_____

_____

_____

Of course, instead of lessening her hatred, this explanation only infuriated Elizabeth. She barely had the courage to read Darcy's defense of his treatment of Wickham. This was more straightforward. The story that Wickham had told Elizabeth was a total fabrication. Wickham received an inheritance upon the death of the older Mr. Darcy and turned down the assignment to a pastorate. He had declared his intention to study law and received an additional large sum to help pay for costs. Wickham quickly spent all the funds on gambling, a deep-seated vice. Wickham's final injury to the Darcy family was his attempt to seduce Darcy's very young sister, Georgianna. He declared to her his love which her inexperienced heart chose to believe. The planned elopement was confessed to her older brother. Darcy sent Wickham away in shame to wallow in his bitter loss, and Georgianna learned the shame of being duped. Wickham was nothing like the wounded gentleman that he had portrayed to Elizabeth.

Her accepting the truth of the second issue made Elizabeth rethink the circumstance concerning her sister. The letter had the desired effect.

Slowly, over many months, Elizabeth allowed the letter to soften her hatred and prejudice of Mr. Darcy. Darcy's conclusion to the letter shows his regard, if somewhat muted: "I hope this letter will lessen your abhorrence of me. I will only add, God bless you." The faithfulness of Darcy's love for Elizabeth is unveiled as the story moves forward. Let's revisit this thought soon.

2 Peter 3:1 speaks of letters, "This is now the second letter that I am writing to you, beloved." Peter reminds his friends of the importance of holy prophecy through a written letter. Letters are powerful and have the opportunity to provide ongoing communication. I believe that Mr. Darcy was wise to use this means of explaining himself to Elizabeth. After understanding the truth about Wickham, she was also able to return to his explanation of separating Jane and Bingley and to read it again with less prejudice.

The art of correspondence is almost lost in these days of technological communication. Do you see the wisdom of using letters to clear up a misunderstanding? _____

Share a time when you either received a letter or wrote a letter to explain yourself.

_____

_____

_____

_____

The famous love-passage in Scripture is 1 Corinthians 13. Verse eight states that "love never _____." True, honest love has the strength to withstand even the most verbal rejection. Elizabeth's unexpected rejection of his overly confident proposal slowed Mr. Darcy down on the outside, but his deep love for her remained buried in his heart. One Jane Austen meme on social media says: "Jane Austen-creating unrealistic expectations since 1811." That is so true; every man should be Mr. Darcy. And every woman should have the opportunity to have a relationship with him.

A final thought is simply to apply the lessons of Mr. Darcy and Elizabeth Bennet to our own lives. Let us be faithful in our love to those entrusted to our care and let us be truly prepared to receive such love from another. Faithful, abiding, simple-hearted love can carry any relationship to a deeper level. Let's focus on loving and being loved.

WEEK FOUR

SECRET #2 ~ A WILLINGNESS TO GROW

Mr. Darcy's decision to be transparent with Elizabeth in his letter, his willingness to expose the weaknesses of his own family, was the catalyst that began to soften Elizabeth's prejudiced heart. No real growth in a relationship can occur without a transparent spirit on the part of both sides.

Elizabeth did not at first read the letter with an open mind. The passage notes: "With a strong prejudice against everything Mr. Darcy might have to say, Elizabeth read the letter. Then she quickly put the letter away, vowing to never read it again."

"In half a minute, it was open again. She reread, with closest attention, the particulars of Wickham's declining the living as a pastor and receiving so considerable a sum as three thousand pounds. Elizabeth was forced to hesitate. She wanted to justify his story with Mr. Darcy's but could not. Wickham's designs on Georgianna Darcy had even been hinted at just yesterday by Colonel Fitzwilliam, Mr. Darcy's cousin."

Then Elizabeth thought back to the day she met George Wickham. "She perfectly remembered everything that passed between them that first evening at Mrs. Philip's, and she was now struck with the impropriety of such communications to a stranger. He had boasted of having no fear of Mr. Darcy yet avoided the Netherfield ball the next week. Further meditation brought her to recognize that Mr. Darcy was esteemed and valued by everyone who knew him, but that Wickham's reputation was known to no one."

All of this pondering led Elizabeth to grow increasingly ashamed of herself, "How despicably I have acted! I, who have prided myself on my discernment! I, who have valued my own abilities. How humiliating is this discovery! Yet how just the humiliation! Vanity has been my folly. Till this moment, I never really knew myself."

Psalm 15:1,2 reveals: "O LORD…Who shall dwell on Your holy hill…He who…speaks the truth in his heart…" A willingness to grow often begins with an honest and transparent heart. Mr. Darcy's wisdom of explaining himself in a letter is working its magic on Elizabeth Bennet's heart. She's softening toward him and censuring herself for her folly and prejudice.

Do you fault Elizabeth for being naïve in her relationship with George Wickham? _____ Have you ever been duped by a conniving individual? _____ Share your story:

_____

_____

_____

_____

In a psalm of David, **Psalm 51:6** the author acknowledges his wrongdoing, and confesses to God: "You delight in truth in the inward being." Like the psalmist Elizabeth is speaking truth to her own soul. A closer, more open-minded scrutiny of Mr. Darcy's explanation concerning his dealings with Wickham forces Elizabeth to see the truth of her own prejudice.

Upon honest reflection, Elizabeth realizes how strange it was for Wickham to share his story of woe on his first opportunity to gain her ear. With her new knowledge, she feels as if Wickham was intentionally influencing her thinking against Mr. Darcy and towards himself. Truth always has the ability to set someone free. In this case, Elizabeth has been freed to think more clearly about Mr. Darcy because of the truth.

John 8:32 has Jesus declaring, "And you will know the _____, and the _____ will set you free." Jesus was speaking of the truth of salvation. But in a broader sense, all truth has the capacity to release a person from the prison of lies and prejudice.

Do you embrace truth for its ability to set one free from the trap of lies? Share a time when receiving the truth has set you free from the snare of lies.

_____

_____

_____

_____

Elizabeth's thoughts soon returned to thinking about Darcy's explanation of separating Jane and Bingley. She decided to read again his account of that.

His account of separating Bingley and Jane at first seemed insufficient, until she read it again. The author said, "Widely different was the effect of the second perusal. Darcy had declared himself totally unsuspicious of Jane's emotional attachment to Bingley." It was only then that Elizabeth remembered Charlotte's opinion that Jane's feelings were too little displayed; Jane had a constant air of complacency in her manners, seldom showing her feelings. Here Elizabeth stopped to absorb the truth of Charlotte's words.

1 Peter 4:8 advises: "-keep loving one another earnestly..." Jane Bennet was modest and very composed. Although she loved deeply, she rarely expressed her emotions in word or attitude. Darcy claimed that he did not think that Jane loved Bingley as much as Bingley loved Jane. Darcy used this belief to motivate him to separate the two.

Do you show the love that you feel? _____ Are you shy or overt with your feelings? _____ Do you blame Darcy for misreading Jane's feeling? _____ Can you share an occasion where you misread someone?

_____

_____

_____

_____

But when Elizabeth came again to that part of the letter where her family was mentioned, she was mortified. Austen says, "Her shame was severe, and she could not deny the truth of the charges. The compliment that Mr. Darcy paid to herself and Jane soothed her spirit, but it could not truly console her. Jane's disappointment had actually been the work of her nearest relations. This knowledge made Elizabeth very depressed." Although truth has the capacity to free someone, it often carries a heavy weight. Sometimes truth needs to be emotionally absorbed before it can begin the work of liberating someone.

Elizabeth had wandered the lanes between Rosings Park and the parsonage for two hours, pouring over the letter. Thinking over it consumed her and demanded decisions. She wondered what she would do with this new information. **Luke 12:48** notes:"…to whom much was given, of him much will be required."

Upon returning to the parsonage, Elizabeth learned that she had missed a visit from Mr. Darcy and Colonel Fitzwilliam. They had stopped to say their good-byes since their visit with their aunt was over. Elizabeth was thankful to have missed them, glad for the opportunity to think uninterrupted.

Only a week later, Elizabeth's visit came to an end. Once she had an opportunity alone with Jane, she shared about Mr. Darcy's proposal, her reaction, and Darcy's letter, but only in his explanation of Wickham. Jane expressed sorrow that Mr. Darcy should have delivered his sentiments in a manner so little suited to recommend them; but more grieved for the unhappiness that Elizabeth's refusal must have given him.

"Indeed, I am heartily sorry for him," Elizabeth said. "But he has other feelings which will probably drive away his regard for me."

Romans 12:2 offers, "-be _____ by the renewal of your _____..." Although this verse is specifically speaking of our transformed life in Christ through the Word, it can apply to other areas of life. The truth that was shared in Darcy's letter is slowly changing Elizabeth's mind. She's already changed from disdain and disrespect to accepting new truths and pity for her rejection of Darcy.

Has your mind ever been changed by accepting a better version of the truth? Share a time when your mind was transformed by receiving more accurate information.

_____

_____

_____

When Elizabeth shared the part of Darcy's letter concerning Wickham, Jane was shocked. Poor Jane would have willingly gone through the world without believing that there was so much wickedness in the whole race of mankind, as were collected in George Wickham. The girls here agreed to not share this new information about George Wickham with family and friends. Their reasoning was that the regiment was soon to leave the neighborhood, and his soiled reputation would harm no one they knew.

Late Spring and early Summer brought changes to the Longbourn home: Lydia had been invited to join Colonel Forster's wife and the regiment at Brighton for the summer; Elizabeth had been invited to do a summer tour with her aunt and uncle as far north as Derbyshire; Jane would have the task of playing with and caring for her nieces and nephews. During these weeks, Elizabeth's mind gradually softened in her thoughts towards Mr. Darcy.

It was discussed that her trip would include a tour of Pemberley, Mr. Darcy's estate. Elizabeth was curious to see exactly what it was that she had missed out on by turning down Darcy's proposal.

Growth, as well as the willingness to grow, can be a painful process. Growth involves stretching and strengthening. In this beautiful tale, we see both Elizabeth and Mr. Darcy allowing themselves the flexibility to engage in both aspects of growth. Elizabeth faced intense pain to admit that she had been duped by Wickham and deep humiliation at the folly of her own family's role in separating Jane and Bingley. Mr. Darcy, too, became stretched as he grew past his self-centeredness and arrogance to continue to love Elizabeth, despite her accusatory rejection. Individual growth lends itself to growth as a couple.

GOD

MAN   **WOMAN**

Above is a relationship triangle. Draw an arrow from man to God, and then from woman to God. As we grow closer to God as individuals, we can also grow closer to each other as a couple.

Are there ways that you can improve a relationship by drawing closer to God? Share one relationship in your life that can be improved by growing closer to God.

_____

_____

_____

A willingness to grow is vital to all thriving relationships. May we embrace the process of becoming that person that we need to be in our lives.

WEEK FIVE

SECRET #3 ~ RESPECT

An online dictionary, Oxford Languages defines respect as a deep admiration for someone elicited by their abilities, qualities, or achievements. It is pretty obvious that Mr. Darcy respected Elizabeth Bennet for nearly all of their acquaintance, but for Elizabeth, the respect only began to grow after she read about Darcy's explanations in his letter.

When Elizabeth was explaining about Darcy's proposal to Jane and the description of George Wickham's evil character, she says: "Mr. Darcy has all the goodness." She acknowledged that Darcy was the truly respectable man of the two.

Her respect becomes more visible when she has an opportunity to chat with George Wickham before the regiment leaves the Meryton area. Elizabeth confessed, "Mr. Darcy improves on acquaintance."

Wickham looked surprised and asked whether he improved in address only, or in essentials. Elizabeth's response alarmed Wickham, as made obvious by his heightened complexion and agitated looks. She said, "In essentials, I believe, he is very much what he ever was. I simply meant that from knowing him better, his disposition was better understood."

Luke 6:45 reminds us, "-for out of the abundance of the heart the mouth speaks." Mr. Darcy, in his letter of explanation, shares the truth from his heart. At first, Elizabeth rejects this truth. But the beauty of a letter is that is can speak repeatedly and work to change a person's mind. She begins to respect Mr. Darcy for the honorable man that he is.

Do you see the power of your words to wound or heal?

_____ Words are indicators of the heart. What do your words say about the condition of your heart?

_____

_____

_____

Mr. Darcy, through the means of a letter, was able to change Elizabeth's mind with the truth. Elizabeth then has the opportunity to share her changed mind with both Jane and Wickham.

How does Wickham react to Elizabeth's endorsement of Darcy?

_____

Do you feel that Elizabeth intentionally brought Darcy up to Wickham?

_____ Have you ever used truth to make someone

uncomfortable? _____ Share this instance.

_____

_____

_____

Respect is truly both internal and external. It often begins in silent contemplation and admiration, but often needs to find a way to be expressed to others. The outward declarations of respect are really a reflection of the heart's belief.

But Elizabeth's respect for Mr. Darcy had only to grow with the opportunity to know him better. When Elizabeth began her summer holiday with her aunt and uncle, she had the chance to see Mr. Darcy's home, Pemberley. When their trip paused in the village of Lambton, where her aunt had spent her childhood, her family expressed again a desire to get a tour of Pemberley mansion. Elizabeth, worried about a chance meeting with

Mr. Darcy, was assured that he was not at home. The three arrived at the mansion eager to know more about it.

The housekeeper gave the tour of the inside of the mansion, which was beautifully situated on well-manicured land. As they passed through rooms, they were given minute details of paintings and furniture. In one, several miniatures were displayed: one obviously of George Wickham.

The housekeeper said: "This is the son of my late master's steward. He was brought up by him at great expense. He is now gone into the army, but I am afraid he has turned out very wild." Elizabeth's aunt and uncle, unaware of Wickham's true nature, were surprised at such a comment. She could not return their look of disbelief.

"And this is a portrait of my master-very like him. Done about eight years ago," the housekeeper pointed out. When her aunt asked her if the likeness was a good one, Elizabeth expressed that it was. The housekeeper's respect of Elizabeth grew with the information that she knew Mr. Darcy. She knew that Mr. Darcy was honorable and only admitted honorable people into his circle of friendship. The housekeeper went on to explain how she had never had a cross word from him her whole life. The housekeeper's commendation further increased Elizabeth's respect of Darcy. Who could easily disregard the admiration of a person who had known this man since his childhood? Elizabeth easily accepted what surprised her family.

Proverbs 15:23 notes, "To make an apt _____ is a _____ to a man, and a word in season, how _____ it is!"

In a simple observation, the housekeeper of Pemberley gave a clear understanding of both the character of Mr. Darcy and the character of George Wickham. Mr. Wickham disdained the generosity of the Darcy family and spurned their offers of help. Mr. Darcy never had a cross word for the housekeeper his whole life.

The housekeeper had an appropriate and good commendation of Mr. Darcy. Why is her praise so valuable?

_____

_____

_____

Do you see the value of praising people you know well? Do you praise people you love to others? Take a moment to share a word of praise about someone that you know very well.

_____

_____

And for the first time, the knowledge that she could have been mistress of Pemberley had she accepted Darcy's proposal, filled Elizabeth with regret. She doubted herself for turning him down. Only the remembrance of his censure of her relations tempered her desire. But the opportunity to know more about him presented itself.

They had finished the tour of the house and had been turned over to the gardener for the tour of the grounds, when Mr. Darcy himself strode up to the group. Elizabeth was mortified. They were within twenty yards of each other before they realized it. Quickly, the cheeks of both were overspread with the deepest blush. The gardener's surprise showed that Mr. Darcy was truly unexpected.

Mr. Darcy made civil inquiries about the health of her immediate family and asked to be introduced to her traveling companions. Elizabeth wondered if he would be surprised to learn that these were some of the relatives that he had disdained, but he heard of their connection without hesitation. He got Mr. Gardiner talking of fishing and soon invited him to fish in his streams. Elizabeth's astonishment was extreme, and she wondered if his politeness stemmed from his still loving her.

Elizabeth's final indication of Mr. Darcy's continued esteem was his asking permission to introduce her to his sister when she arrived the next day. For the rest of the day, her thoughts swung between the mortification of being caught on his grounds to wondering at his being so polite to her and her family. Did he still love her? This thought only increased her respect of him. His ability to love her despite her rejection, and his obvious regard did much to grow her admiration.

1 Corinthians 13:7 declares, "Love bears _____ things, believes _____ things, hopes all things, endures _____ things." That Mr. Darcy's love and respect for Elizabeth had not changed despite her initial rejection of him is obvious to even the casual reader. He openly asks to be introduced to her family and requests the chance to introduce his sister to Elizabeth.

Do you believe that Mr. Darcy still faithfully loves and respects Elizabeth? _____ Do you faithfully love others despite personal insults or wounds? _____

Share an example of your faithful love for someone and/or their faithful love for you.

_____

_____

It seems that the love chapter in the Bible knows Mr. Darcy well when it says, "Charity (love in action) never fails." (King James Version) Darcy was expressing his enduring love by overcoming the weaknesses that had originally caused Elizabeth to reject him in the first place. His ability to grow and change prompted Elizabeth's own transformation.

The next morning at the inn, Mr. Darcy arrived with his sister, Georgianna, and Mr. Bingley. He took the opportunity to introduce his sister to her, and Bingley inquired after her family. Elizabeth was pleased to meet Darcy's sister, and found her extremely shy, rather than proud as Mr. Wickham had described her. She could hardly speak to Elizabeth beyond one-syllable words, but she managed to invite her and her family to dine the next day.

Elizabeth spent hours after the visit thinking over everything. That Mr. Darcy still loved her was obvious: his desire to introduce his sister to her and his including Bingley in the visit proved that. Above her growing respect and esteem for him, there was a growing goodwill within her. Realizing that the immense change in Darcy was due to his unfailing love for her, Elizabeth found herself grateful to him and had a real interest in his welfare. She wondered if she should employ her powers to bring about a renewal of his proposal.

Philippians 2:4 offers, "Let each of you look _____ _____ to his own interests, but also to the interests _____ _____."

Mr. Darcy's enduring love and respect for Elizabeth is growing her love and respect for him. She longs for his well-being and desires to live for his welfare.

If you're familiar with the story, did you believe that Mr. Darcy would propose a second time here if given the right circumstance? _____ Does Elizabeth express a growing respect for Mr. Darcy? _____ If yes, give your thoughts on how this is evident.

_____

_____

_____

Can you share an example of how someone's faithfulness to you changed your perspective or attitude?

_____

_____

_____

Song of Solomon offers a look at a beautiful love story. Look up chapter eight verse six and complete the reference: "Set me as a seal up your heart, as a seal upon your arm, for _____ is as strong as _____..." As strong as death is to eternally separate, love is even stronger. Mr. Darcy's solid love and respect for Elizabeth is growing her love and respect for him. She knew that an opportunity to receive Mr. Darcy's proposal a second time was a real possibility if the opportunity arose. Respect truly is the standard that protects tender love through its gentle guidance.

Take a moment to reflect: how can you cultivate the respect of others? Since it's integral to relationships, how can respect be earned?

_____
_____
_____
_____
_____
_____
_____

WEEK SIX

SECRET #4 ~ CONFESSION

The visit to Pemberley the next day was good. Upon their leaving, Caroline Bingley thought she would engage Mr. Darcy's attention by criticizing Elizabeth's looks: "I would not have known her. She is so brown and coarse!"

"That is no miraculous consequence of traveling in summer," Darcy defended.

"For my part," Caroline returned, "I could never see any beauty in her. Even her so-called fine eyes appear shrewd to me. She has a self-sufficiency without fashion that is intolerable. Even you, Darcy, disliked her looks when you first met her."

"Yes, but that was only when I first met her. It has been many months since I have considered Elizabeth Bennet one of the handsomest women of my acquaintance," he replied.

Sadly, Caroline's attempt to belittle Elizabeth backfired.

Proverbs 21:23 has some advice that could have helped Caroline Bingley: "Whoever keeps his mouth and his tongue keeps himself out of trouble." Poor Caroline! Her attempt to draw Darcy's attention away from Elizabeth and towards herself did not have the desired result. Instead of obtaining the compliment for which she was fishing, she was further wounded by Darcy's praise of Elizabeth's looks.

Was Darcy tricked by Caroline's attempt to draw him into a bit of gossip? _____ Caroline should have been wise enough to see that this sort of debasing gossip would turn against her. Have you ever engaged in gossip only to have it turn on you? _____ If you are comfortable, share the experience.

_____

_____

_____

The next morning, Elizabeth received two letters from Jane while her aunt and uncle were out for a walk. The distressing news changed the course of the day: Lydia had run away from the camp in Brighton with George Wickham! The letter stated that the original plan was for them to travel to Scotland to elope and be officially married, but that they had been traced no further than London. The family's disgrace was complete! No honorable young man would be eager to be attached to any of the daughters in marriage after such a lack of propriety on the part of one sister.

Just then Mr. Darcy walked through the door for a visit.

Elizabeth's horror and distress were so fresh that it could not be hidden. She confessed the news to Mr. Darcy and her regrets of not informing her family of the evil of Wickham's character. Darcy, worried for Elizabeth's health, sent a servant to look for the Gardiners.

"Wretched! Wretched! What a mistake," Elizabeth moaned. "I could have prevented this had I exposed what I knew of his faults."

Darcy made no answer but paced the room silently. Elizabeth instantly understood that her power over him was sinking under such proof of family weakness and disgrace. Elizabeth recognized that she could never have honestly felt love for Mr. Darcy, until now, when all love was vain and beyond hope. Mr. Darcy assured her of his secrecy, telling no one of the family's disgrace, and asked to be dismissed.

Elizabeth felt it probable that she would never see him again. She understood that both gratitude and esteem were good foundations for love:

both swelled within her while she realized what could have been, had it not been for Lydia's foolish, self-centered behavior.

James 5:16 counsels, "-confess your sins to one another and pray for one another, that you may be _____."

Although the circumstances of Darcy's arriving just as Elizabeth was learning of Lydia's disgraceful and foolish decision rather forces her to confess everything to him, Elizabeth's deep and transparent acknowledgement of her part is tender and beautiful. James encourages people to confess their sins and weaknesses to each other. This first honest step leads to healing.

Do you believe that Elizabeth's confession softens or hardens Darcy's heart? _____ Does Elizabeth realize what she lost as a result of Lydia's actions? _____ Have you ever realized the truth of a relationship only after the connection had been severed? _____ Why is it that as humans we rarely appreciate what we have until it's too late?

_____
_____
_____
_____

Darcy left, and her aunt and uncle arrived to prepare a return trip home to remedy the disgrace to the family.

Elizabeth here utilizes confession with Mr. Darcy, though maybe he should get the credit for being honest first with his letter. He risked exposing the account of Georgianna's nearly being seduced by his old enemy, George Wickham. Although, likely done in anger and an opportunity to justify himself at the time, the result was positive. It got Elizabeth considering Mr. Darcy in a different light, looking at him with a more open mind. But Elizabeth took a greater risk with her confession.

Elizabeth understood that the shame of Lydia's behavior could not be long hidden from public scrutiny. And Mr. Darcy's sudden arrival just after her learning of the situation, hardly gave her any other choice. But still, confession is good for the soul and good for relationships as well. It would be more likely that confessing an ugly situation could soften the heart of the listener. If Mr. Darcy had heard the account from a third party, he would not have had the opportunity to see how the news had devastated Elizabeth. Although she did not know it at the time, her distress moved him more to action than to disdain.

1 Corinthians 13:6 speaks of solid love when it says, love "does not rejoice at wrongdoing, but rejoices with the _____." Mr. Darcy is an honorable man. He loves Elizabeth Bennet. Her heart-felt confession touches him like nothing else before. It moves him to accurately view Lydia and Wickham as the wrongdoers and Elizabeth as the victim of the fallout of their decision.

How is Darcy's behavior influenced by viewing the situation through loving eyes?

_____

_____

_____

Has love ever influenced the way you received a confession? Share a time when love motivated you to forgive and seek the good of another.

_____

_____

_____

_____

Jane Austen's novel contains a few more confessions, but we will save Mr. Darcy's grand confession toward the end for the last secret.

After returning to Longbourn, Elizabeth, and her aunt and uncle settle in to learn the details of Lydia's plight. Mr. Bennet was in London searching for the pair, and Mr. Gardiner promised to join him there the next day. The plan was to find Lydia and Wickham, and if they were not married, to make the necessary arrangements to bring about the marriage.

Mr. Bennet returned home, and sooner than could be believed, a letter arrived from their uncle saying that the couple had been discovered. Mr. Gardiner had made the necessary financial commitments to get George Wickham to agree to a marriage with Lydia. Mr. Bennet was worried that he could never repay Uncle Gardiner for the amount needed to create such a happy conclusion.

Once the couple were married, they were granted permission to visit the Bennet family before moving to the north of England where Wickham had received a new post in the militia. The day for the visit arrived. A smile decked the face of Mrs. Bennet as the carriage was heard to pull up; her husband looked grave; the daughters alarmed, anxious, and uneasy. How would the couple behave that had brought so much shame upon the family? If the Bennet family was hoping for a humble confession and apology, they were about to be very disappointed. Lydia and Wickham entered the room, where they were welcomed with rapture and joy by Mrs. Bennet. Mr. Bennet's countenance gained in austerity, and he barley opened his lips. Elizabeth was disgusted by the easy assurance of the young couple, and Jane was shocked. Elizabeth blushed; Jane blushed; but the cheeks of the two who caused the confusion remained unchanged.

The confession and repentance needed to mend the rift in the Bennet family would never be uttered, as the two needing to confess had hardened hearts. Lydia and Wickham settled into the family as if they had married honorably, even bold in their self-assurance.

2 Timothy 3:2 speaks of Lydia and Wickham, "For people will be lovers of self, lovers of money, proud, arrogant, abusive, disobedient to parents, ungrateful, unholy…"

With no shame for their behavior, with no gratitude for the role that others played in patching up a marriage, Lydia and Wickham arrive home at Longbourn to visit the family with only pride and arrogance. The other daughters blush to think of all the shame that the two brought on the family, but the one who should have blushed was brazen.

Have you ever encountered someone like Lydia who was brazen in their sinful choices? Were you able to manage their arrogant attitude or did you find it difficult to endure?

_____

_____

_____

_____

But something happened that would change the events of the future of the family: Lydia told the story of her wedding and accidently revealed a secret. She told, "The day of the wedding arrived, and I was in such a fuss! And there was my aunt, all the time I was dressing, preaching away as if she was reading a sermon. I heard not one word in ten, of course, for I was thinking of my dear Wickham. We breakfasted. My uncle went out on business but came back on time. Upon arriving at the church, we met the small party, and of course, Mr. Darcy."

"Mr. Darcy!" Elizabeth exclaimed. "Why was he there?"

"Oh yes! He came to be with Wickham. Gracious me, I forgot! That was to remain a secret; I forgot! And I promised so faithfully, too. What will Wickham say?" she asked.

Although this was not the confession that Elizabeth was expecting, it was the one that prompted a new set of circumstances. Elizabeth, eager to learn why Mr. Darcy had attended Lydia's wedding, quickly wrote to her aunt asking for an explanation. The answer was a surprise to Elizabeth.

Parts of Aunt Gardiner's answer went like this:

"My Dear Niece,

I shall devote the whole morning to answering your letter, but I must confess myself a little surprised. I did not imagine such inquiries would be necessary on your side. Your uncle is just as surprised as I am. On the day I returned to London, Mr. Darcy had visited with your uncle for several hours. He had left Derbyshire a day after we did with the express purpose of finding Lydia and Wickham. His meeting was to report that he had.

Mr. Darcy had blamed himself for the situation, having had too much pride to expose Wickham's true character. Darcy had been forced to bribery to obtain the whereabouts of the couple. He visited them several times and attempted to get Lydia to leave with him. But Lydia was resolute: she did not care about her family and friends and did not want his help. Wickham on the other hand, was willing to accept help. He wanted more from Darcy than he would get, but it was Mr. Darcy who did everything. He paid Wickham's gambling debts of about a thousand pounds, placed a thousand pounds on the settlement of Lydia, and purchased his new commission in the north of England. Darcy insisted on carrying all the financial burden, but he also insisted that your uncle take the credit for it. He then returned to Pemberley and only came back the day of the wedding to assure that Wickham would keep his end of the bargain.

I fancy, Elizabeth, that obstinacy is the real defect of Mr. Darcy's character. But otherwise, I must confess that his behavior, understanding, and opinions all please me. Finally, let me say that I look forward to a tour of the whole of Pemberley Park, once you are settled there. A low carriage and ponies will do.

Most sincerely yours, M Gardiner."

Again **1 Corinthians 13:8** is revealed "_____ _____ _____."
Mr. Darcy did it all! And he did it all because of his solid and passionate love for Elizabeth. When Elizabeth writes her aunt for an explanation of why Darcy was at Lydia's wedding, the aunt is surprised. She assumed that Elizabeth knew of Darcy's role in patching up Lydia and Wickham's scandalous decision. Elizabeth is humbled and grateful.

Did Darcy display solid and enduring love for Elizabeth, using this to motivate him to fix the scandal? _____ Do you believe that love was Darcy's motivation? _____ Describe Darcy's love for Elizabeth in a few sentences.

_____

_____

_____

_____

Needless to say, this confession of Mr. Darcy's role in repairing the shameful affair of Lydia and Wickham threw Elizabeth into a flutter of spirits, in which it was difficult to say whether pleasure or pain bore the greatest share. Mr. Darcy still loved her! It could be the only explanation for him placing himself through the horror of hunting down the wayward couple and fixing things to remove the shame.

This confession, shared by her aunt, gave Elizabeth a jumble of thoughts and emotions. The Gardiners assumed that Elizabeth was fully aware of Mr. Darcy's deeds, as well as aware of his motives. They believed only a deep love for their niece was the prompt that caused Mr. Darcy to humiliate himself and intervene in the lives of Lydia and Wickham.

The final confession I will save for the last secret. Mr. Darcy gets the prize for the most improved man in English literature when he confesses all Elizabeth did to awaken his better self.

Confession is a beautiful tool that should be used often to keep a relationship fresh. It allows the confessor to practice humility and appeal, and the listener to practice grace and forgiveness. May we give confession its proper respect as the reset button for true friendship.

WEEK SEVEN

SECRET #5 ~ GRATITUDE

Truly, gratitude gets the final credit for changing the course of the relationship between Mr. Darcy and Elizabeth. Elizabeth has the opportunity to express her appreciation to Mr. Darcy.

After making amends for his pride by mending the reputations of Lydia and Wickham, Mr. Darcy then fixed the other mistake he had made: that of separating his friend Charles Bingley from Elizabeth's sister, Jane. He did this by apologizing to Bingley for his role in the separation, and even confessed that he had known of Jane's presence in London the previous winter and purposefully kept it from him.

Of course, Bingley was very angry, but being also modest, he accepted Darcy's apology and acknowledgement that Jane Bennet actually loved him. Bingley even went so far as to ask his friend's blessing on pursuing Jane. Mr. Darcy laughed and asked, "Do you need my blessing?"

Soon the Bennet's neighborhood was abuzz with the news that Mr. Bingley was returning there for the hunting season. On the day of his arrival, he paid a visit to the Bennet home with Darcy. Both Elizabeth and Jane were unsettled when the housekeeper announced their arrival; both blushed deeply when the men entered the drawing room.

The meeting between the two couples was intensely awkward, but Mrs. Bennet's folly of doting on Bingley and nearly ignoring Darcy carried the mortification of the meeting into the shame of her conversation. After the initial visit, Bingley came every day to spend time with Jane and the family. Mr. Darcy had left the neighborhood to attend to business, content with having created the opportunity for his friend to propose.

Proverbs 28:13 remind us, "Whoever conceals his _____ will not _____, but he who _____ and _____ them will obtain _____."

Mr. Darcy is remarkably changed! Not only does he confess his interference and deception to his friend, Charles Bingley, but he also works out the circumstances for his friend to reconnect with Jane Bennet. He's forgiven by Bingley and heartily gives his blessing on a union.

Do you believe that Mr. Darcy's change of heart goes beyond that of an ordinary apology? _____ Do you believe that Mr. Bingley asked for Darcy's blessings out of a sense of modesty? _____

Have you ever given or received such an obvious confession or seen such a change of heart in a person? If you are comfortable, write their name and share the example.

_____

_____

_____

_____

Elizabeth was disappointed by the lack of attention she had received from Darcy on this occasion. She knew herself enough to know that her opinion of Mr. Darcy had done a complete about face since the spring. She knew she loved him and longed to thank him for fixing the mess of Lydia's poor choices.

The chance to do this was brought about by Darcy's aunt, Lady Catherine de Bourgh. Through some gossip source running through the Hunsford neighborhood, Lady Catherine had heard that Elizabeth was soon to be engaged to Mr. Darcy. She immediately set out for the Bennet's home at Longbourn to express her opinion on such a union.

Her arrival created a stir, but when she addressed herself to Elizabeth, and asked for a bit of privacy to speak, everyone was surprised. She began: "A report of you being united with my own nephew, Mr. Darcy, is being circulated about. I know it must be a scandalous falsehood, but I resolved to instantly set off for this place and make my sentiments known!"

"If you believe that it is impossible to be true, I wonder that you took the trouble of coming so far. Your coming to Longbourn will be rather a confirmation of the report, if such truly exists. I never heard of it," Elizabeth responded.

"Mr. Darcy is engaged to my daughter!" Lady Catherine exclaimed. "It was planned from their infancy. Are you lost to every feeling of propriety and delicacy? Honor, decorum, prudence, and interest forbid such a union between you and my nephew! You will be censured, slighted, and despised by everyone connected with him," she threatened. "Tell me at once, are you engaged to him?"

"I am not," Elizabeth replied.

"And will you promise to never enter into such an engagement?"

"I will make no promise of the kind. You have insulted me in every possible method. I must beg return to the house," Elizabeth retorted.

Lady Catherine followed her back to the house, arguing as she went. She entered her carriage in an outrage and refused to send best wishes to Elizabeth's mother.

Look up Proverbs 13:10 and write it here: _____ _____ _____ _____ _____ _____, _____ _____ _____ _____ _____ _____ _____ _____. Lady Catherine's arrogance prompts her to make a trip to Longbourn to threaten Elizabeth Bennet. An unnamed gossip in the Hunsford area is spreading the news that Darcy and Elizabeth will soon be engaged. Lady Catherine de Bourgh insolently makes her sentiments known to Elizabeth.

Have you ever known or conversed with a person as proud as Lady de Bourgh? _____ Do You believe that Elizabeth handled the tirade with both courtesy and courage? _____ Share a time when you used wisdom to contend with a proud person.

_____

_____

_____

News of this heated exchange was the encouragement that Mr. Darcy needed. When his aunt stopped by his place in London on her way home, and told him of Elizabeth's response to her tirade, it had quite the opposite effect than what she had intended. It caused Mr. Darcy to hope that Elizabeth had changed her mind about him.

He set off the next morning to return to Bingley's home, seeking an opportunity to speak to Elizabeth alone. He arrived with Bingley at the Bennet home only two days after the engagement of his friend to Jane. A walk was quickly proposed, and the group set off: Kitty veered off to say hello to Mariah Lucas, and Jane and Bingley lagged behind. Soon Mr. Darcy and Elizabeth were walking alone.

Elizabeth began: "Mr. Darcy, I am a very selfish creature! I can no longer help thanking you for your unexampled kindness to my poor sister, Lydia. Ever since I have known it, I have been most anxious to acknowledge to you how grateful I feel. I express my gratitude for my family also, for they do not know."

"I am exceedingly sorry," Darcy replied, "that you have been informed of it. I did not think that Mrs. Gardiner was so little to be trusted."

"You must not blame my aunt. Lydia's thoughtlessness first betrayed it to me, and I could not rest until I knew the particulars."

Mr. Darcy responded, "If you will thank me, let it be for yourself alone. Your family owes me nothing. Much as I respect them, I believe, I thought only of you. Elizabeth, you are too generous to trifle with me. If your feelings are still what they were last April, tell me at once. My affections and wishes are unchanged, but one word from you will silence me on this subject forever."

Jane Austen shares, "Elizabeth, feeling the anxiety of Mr. Darcy's situation, forced herself to speak quickly. She told him that her feelings had undergone so material a change, as to make her receive with gratitude and pleasure his present assurances. The happiness which her reply produced was such as he had never felt before, and he expressed himself as warmly as a man violently in love can be supposed to do. Had Elizabeth looked up and encountered his eye, she might have seen his expression of heartfelt delight diffusing over his face, making him more handsome than ever."

1 Corinthians 13:13 concludes, "So now faith, hope, and love abide, these three; but the _____ of these is _____."

Gratitude wins the day! As Elizabeth has an opportunity to thank Mr. Darcy for all that he did to mend Lydia's soiled reputation, love feels strengthened enough for Mr. Darcy to propose a second time. The results were beautiful!

Do you believe that gratitude worked out the circumstances for Darcy to propose a second time? Explain why or why not you believe this.

_____

_____

_____

Do you believe that enduring love, like that of Mr. Darcy, has the power to outlast rejection? _____ Can you share a story of how love won out in the end?

_____

_____

_____

Their walk continued, but neither of them were paying attention to the direction. Elizabeth's desire to express her gratitude to Mr. Darcy was the encouragement he needed to propose a second time. And Elizabeth's positive response changed their future. Mr. Darcy shared how his aunt's interference influenced their happy circumstances.

"It taught me to hope as I had scarcely allowed myself to hope before. I knew enough of your disposition to be certain, that, had you absolutely, irrevocably decided against me, you would have acknowledged it to my aunt frankly and openly."

Elizabeth colored and laughed, "Yes, you know enough of my frankness to believe me capable of that. After abusing you so abominably to your face, I could have no scruple in abusing you to all your relations."

"What did you say to me that I did not deserve?" Darcy challenged. "The recollection of what I said to you that first proposal, my conduct, manners, and expressions are inexpressibly painful to me. Your reproof I shall never forget, 'Had you behaved yourself in a more gentlemen like manner,' tortured me. I hope my letter soon made you think better of me."

Elizabeth explained how the letter gradually helped to remove all her former prejudices.

Darcy confessed humbly, "I am different today because of you. I was taught good principles but attempted to follow them in pride and conceit. My parents, though good themselves, allowed me to be selfish and overbearing, to care for none beyond my family circle, to think meanly of all the rest of the world. Such I would still be had it not been for you, dearest, loveliest Elizabeth! What do I not owe you! You taught me a lesson; hard indeed, at first, but most advantageous. You showed me how insufficient all my schemes were to please a worthy woman."

Humility, the willingness to change and grow, and gratitude all weaved together in the lives of Mr. Darcy and Elizabeth Bennet to create a new and joy-filled future for them.

1 Peter 5:6 shares this truth, "Humble yourselves, therefore, under the _____ _____ of God so that at the _____ time He may _____ you." Mr. Darcy humbly explains to Elizabeth how her first rejection completely humbled and changed him. His humility allowed him to learn the truth about himself. This beautiful transformation came about through pain, confession, and transparency. The happy results came through respect and gratitude.

Do you believe that Darcy gets the credit for the most transformed character in British literature? _____ Do you feel that love mixed with humility and a willingness to grow brought about this change? _____

How have you employed *personal humility* to make changes in your own life?

_____

_____

_____

    Their engagement surprised and pleased the Bennet family. Jane and Bingley were excited to share the freshness of new love with Darcy and Elizabeth. Mr. Bennet expressed that although Mr. Darcy began as proud and conceited, his changed demeanor put him at ease when giving his consent to the marriage. Mrs. Bennet was ever foolish, only expressing joy at how rich Elizabeth would be. The Gardiners were excited to admit Darcy into the family circle and thankful for their part in bringing the two together by bringing Elizabeth on that trip to Pemberley. Only Lady Catherine was outraged by the news.

Gratitude is the expressed joy of any solid relationship. Joy in both the character and actions of the other. Gratitude begins as an attitude of the heart and matures as an expression of the spoken (or even written) word.

CONCLUSION

Now truly, can these facets of a good relationship be counted as secrets? Everyone knows how vital faithful love is to any relationship. True fidelity and loyalty softened by genuine love for another is the bedrock of any communion. Being willing to grow and change allows a connection with another human to morph into beautiful intimacy, knowing things unknown to any other being on the planet. Respect is paramount to solid communication. How can love mature when there is no respect to protect it? Confession is necessary to mend the wounds of the lack of respect. Confession humbles the confessor and tenderizes the one receiving the apology. Finally, gratitude has the opportunity to express the love it feels for the other's tender care and actions. No, these are not secrets. But being reminded of such facets that can contribute to a beautiful relationship and can be the needed boost to start, restart, or jump start a union between two souls.

ABOUT THE AUTHOR

Chrisann has been writing her whole life. As a child, she started hundreds of stories that she never finished.

She has taught high school English Grammar and Composition for more than twenty years and was blessed by the opportunity to teach English as a second language in the Congo, Africa through the Lingala language.

Chrisann is now finishing her stories. Lots of them. Shine-A-Light Press will be publishing her trilogy of novels inspired by her time in the Congo in 2021.
She has three adult children and currently lives in Northern Arizona with her husband, Gale.